HEARTS OF GOLD

Reflections of

INCLUSION

Gold Award Girl Scouts

Sheryl M Robinson

Copyright Page

Published by Grow and Share Network, LLC
First Edition, 2026

ISBN: 978-1-972135-04-4

Printed in the United States of America

Books in the Hearts of Gold Series

- *Earth Guardian*
- *STEM*
- *Creative Voice*
- *Health*
- *Inclusion*
- *Advocacy*
- *Community Connector*

Table of Contents

CHAPTER 1 — Space for Everyone
CHAPTER 2 — Grow Healthy
CHAPTER 3 — The Flavor of Home
CHAPTER 4 — The Voice of Courage
CHAPTER 5 — A Boutique for Belonging
CHAPTER 6 — Colors of Strength
CHAPTER 7 — Class of Kindness
CHAPTER 8 — 1% Awareness Mission
CHAPTER 9 — Sensory Friendly Futures
CHAPTER 10 — Whatever the Obstacle
CHAPTER 11 — World Behind the Blur
CHAPTER 12 — Project Save the Girl Child
CHAPTER 13 — Heart of Belonging

Acknowledgements
About the Author
More Stories

Chapter 1
Space for Everyone

Noticing What's Unseen

If you look around your school, your community, or your own neighborhood, you might notice things that feel unfinished or unfair. Perhaps it is a story that no one talks about, a group of people who seem invisible even though they are right there, or a barrier that prevents someone from joining the fun. To a leader for inclusion, these moments are not accidents; they are signals. They are clues that someone is being left behind and that something important is waiting to be noticed.

In this book, you will meet Gold Award Girl Scouts who refused to be bystanders when they encountered a silence or a taboo subject. They realized that a community is only truly strong when every person in it has a seat at the table. These girls used their curiosity to lean into moments that felt confusing or unfinished, and that choice made all the difference. They learned that leadership doesn't always require being the loudest person in the room; sometimes it means holding a microphone for someone else.

Heart of Inclusion: Empathy

Inclusion is more than just an invitation; it is the act of ensuring that every individual is seen, heard, and respected for exactly who they are. It is about building bridges of belonging where walls once stood. Throughout these chapters, you will see that these projects didn't start with grand speeches or expert knowledge. They started by listening to neighbors, family members, and sometimes to the silence itself.

These leaders recognized that to help a community, they had to understand its lived experience. By stepping into someone else's shoes, they learned that representation matters. Whether it was ensuring a neurodivergent student felt regulated and comfortable or helping a foster teen shop with "their head held high," these girls proved that when people see themselves reflected in their community, they no longer feel alone.

Breaking the Silence of Stigma

Many of the leaders in this book focused on topics that others avoided because they felt uncomfortable or complicated. They used their voices to shine a light on hidden histories and cultural secrets.

You will read about Aanya, who was once scared to eat Indian food in front of her friends but chose to write a book to ensure no other child had to hide their heritage. You'll meet Madison, who saw the heavy, unspoken weight of mental health struggles in minority communities during a global pandemic and created a virtual soapbox to start much-needed conversations. You will also learn about Himani, who tackled the global crisis of gendercide against girls, advocating for the girl child and proving that every daughter has as much potential as any son. These girls discovered that even a small spark of realization can turn into a mission for global change.

Designing for Dignity

Inclusion also means looking at the physical and social barriers that hold people back. It requires a go-getter attitude to push through a mountain of red tape to ensure accessibility for all.

In these pages, you will meet Sofia, who designed a high-end boutique for belonging so that foster youth could find formal wear without the stigma of disclosing their status. You'll meet Lia, who was diagnosed with autism and created fidget bins to provide Sensory Friendly Futures in public spaces. You'll read about Margaret and Rebekkah, who turned their own physical and visual challenges into movements of empathy, proving that a disability never means a lack of ambition. These leaders learned that "whatever the obstacle, we will overcome it".

Built to Lead

Using your voice for good is a marathon of success that requires a blend of passion and strategy. These stories reveal a professional roadmap for change, showing that real leadership involves:

- **Identifying the Gap**: Looking for the silence or the taboo subject others ignore.

- **Building a Dream Team**: Realizing it is okay to ask for help and partnering with experts like doctors, park rangers, and principals.

- **Persevering Through Failure**: Staying calm when a hydroponic wall leaks, a website glitch happens, or a school administration says no.

Through this process, the girls themselves changed. They shifted from quiet, shy to vocal hustlers who know their worth. They discovered that "the more time and energy you put into your project, the more you're going to change as a person".

Your Journey Begins Here

As you journey through these chapters, think about your own big why. You are not a bystander in your community; you are a vital, life-saving source of information waiting to be released.

- Is there a silence in your school that needs to be broken?

- Is there a unique flavor of your culture you want to share?

- Is there someone sitting alone who just needs a bridge of hope?

Whatever makes your heart settle on change is what should drive your next steps. You don't need to be an expert to start; you just need the courage to click send on that first email and the passion to see it through.

The world is a tapestry of transformation, and your voice is a vital thread. It is time to find your own creative voice and turn your passion into a standing ovation that changes the world.

Chapter 2
Grow Healthy

Anna Shinohara (Ep 41)

The Root Of A Healthy Idea

Anna Shinohara was a girl who understood that being a leader meant looking beneath the surface of a problem to find its true cause. Long before she began her project, she had established herself as a dedicated student and athlete in her Michigan community. Whether she was challenging herself on the diving board or playing the viola in her school orchestra, Anna was used to the discipline required to reach a goal. She loved the team atmosphere of diving and the music her orchestra made, but she felt a deep pull toward a different kind of service, one that focused on the health and well-being of the next generation.

Her journey toward her Gold Award project, titled Go Grow Healthy, began with a simple yet startling observation. Anna recognized that many children in her community were suffering from nutritional deficiencies, but the problem wasn't just a lack of food; it was a lack of knowledge about healthy eating. She realized that if children didn't learn how to fuel their bodies correctly while they were young, those poor habits would follow them into adulthood. Anna wanted to create an interactive way to inspire elementary students to choose vegetables over junk food, helping them develop lifelong healthy habits.

This wasn't Anna's first time using science to help the environment or her community. As a younger girl, she had visited a recycling plant for her Bronze Award, where she learned to sift through nets to make handmade paper. For her Silver Award, she took on a much colder challenge: researching the best way to melt snow in Michigan winters without harming the earth. She and her team tested alternatives, including sugar beet juice and salt, and eventually discovered that salt was harmful to the living organisms in local ecosystems. These earlier experiences gave her the confidence to tackle a project that would combine technology, education, and nutrition. She knew that to make a real difference, she couldn't just hand out pamphlets; she had to get the children's hands into the dirt, or, in her case, into the water.

Building The Dream Team

Anna knew that an idea as big as Go Grow Healthy required a support system that stretched across her entire school district. She didn't want to be the only person working on the project because she realized that "it's okay to reach out to people and ask others for help because you're not the only person in this project". Her first major step was finding the right partners to turn her vision of a high-tech garden into a reality. She approached the principal of a local elementary school, Mr. David Ascher, who became a key part of her team, guiding her through the logistics of working with younger students.

To fund the most exciting part of her project, a hydroponic wall garden, Anna had to step into the world of grant writing. This is a professional challenge that many high schoolers never experience. With the help of Mr. Ascher and Larry Antonelli, a representative from the Meemic Foundation, Anna successfully secured the funding needed to purchase the specialized equipment. She also reached out to experts in the field of health. She partnered with Miss Lisa Verdejo, a professional nutritionist, who taught Anna the best ways to present complex nutritional material to children so they would stay engaged and excited.

Anna also realized that her peers could be a powerful tool for change. She collaborated with the high school garden club and a former teacher, Miss Stacy Tanner, who worked with a gardening group at the elementary school. This network of adults and students provided the teamwork and expertise needed to manage the project. Anna also made sure to include Miss Evol Gazzarato, the school district's food director, to ensure her project aligned with the meals served in the cafeteria. By the time the planning phase was complete, Anna had transformed from a student with an idea into the manager of a professional-grade health initiative. She felt empowered knowing that she had a team to support her every step of the way.

High-Tech Harvests And Balanced Plates

The most visual and exciting part of Go Grow Healthy was the installation of the hydroponic wall garden. For many of the elementary students, this was like something out of a science fiction movie. A hydroponic garden grows herbs and vegetables with only water, so there is no soil. The plants receive all their nutrients through a specialized water system, allowing them to grow indoors regardless of the harsh Michigan winter outside. Anna worked closely with the school's gardening group to set up the system and teach them how to care for the herbs and vegetables as they grew.

Anna didn't just want the kids to look at the plants; she wanted them to understand how those vegetables fit into a healthy life. She organized interactive lessons that brought high schoolers and elementary students together. They used the MyPlate food guide to visualize a balanced meal. To keep the project organized and to ensure it was repeatable in the future, Anna utilized several specific strategies and resources during her execution:

- Hydroponic Installation: She set up the vertical water-based garden to provide a year-round source of fresh herbs and vegetables for the school.

- The Plate Activity: She led a hands-on workshop where students drew examples of healthy foods on paper plates to learn about the different food groups.

- Cooking Demonstrations: She collaborated with school chefs to show students how to turn fresh ingredients into tasty, healthy snacks, such as salsa.

- Digital Resource Library: She created a comprehensive Google folder filled with activity ideas and resources so teachers could continue the lessons after she left.

Many students' favorite part was the MyPlate activity. Anna watched as the younger kids drew their favorite fruits and vegetables and even remembered to include the dairy portion on the back of the plate. She was taking the lessons she had learned from her nutritionist advisor and translating them into a language that kids could understand. Her project was no longer just a plan on a laptop; it was a living, breathing classroom where students were discovering that healthy food could be both interesting and high-tech.

Troubleshooting The Wall

Even with a grant and a team of experts, Anna's project hit a major roadblock that tested her patience and resolve. The hydroponic wall garden, which was the centerpiece of her entire mission, turned out to be much more fragile than she expected. Purchasing it from an outside company, Anna assumed it would work perfectly once installed. Instead, the system kept breaking down. "We actually had to replace it three times," Anna recalled, a process that could have easily made her want to give up on the high-tech aspect of the project.

Instead of letting the broken equipment stop her, Anna used it as an opportunity to grow her communication and problem-solving skills. She worked with the company to arrange the replacements and investigated why the system wasn't holding up. But the mechanical issues weren't the only challenge. Once the garden was finally stable, the plants themselves had trouble growing. Anna had to troubleshoot with the gardening group and collaborate even more closely with the elementary students to figure out the right balance of nutrients and light.

This struggle taught Anna a vital lesson about leadership: things will rarely go exactly as planned, and that is where the real learning happens. She realized that being a leader meant being the person who stays calm when the wall is leaking or the plants are wilting. She had to manage her time effectively between her diving practice and her viola rehearsals to ensure she was available to help the students at the elementary school. This experience "helped me break out of my shell a little bit" and made her realize that she could handle professional-level setbacks with grace. By the time the garden was flourishing, Anna had proven that her determination was even stronger than the technology she was using.

The Salsa Celebration and Future Healing

The culmination of Anna's hard work was a high-energy cooking demonstration that brought the whole project together. She worked with the school chefs and the district food director to organize two sessions where students from many different grades came down to the cafeteria. They watched with wide eyes as the chefs showed them how to make salsa with healthy ingredients. After learning about the benefits of fresh vegetables, the kids finally got to taste the results. Even though the salsa was a bit spicy, Anna was thrilled to see that the children enjoyed it.

The success of the Go Grow Healthy project was visible in the 400 people Anna impacted through her keynote speaking and the hundreds of students who now had access to the hydroponic garden. Anna felt a connection with the adults and students she worked with, realizing that her voice could inspire change. The project changed her path, too. As she prepared to attend the University of Michigan, she knew she wanted to take her passion for health to the next level. Her goal is to become a doctor, specifically in cardiology, so she can continue helping people live long, healthy lives.

Reflecting on her years of service, Anna realized that the most rewarding part wasn't just the finished garden, but the confidence she gained. Her advice to others is to find your passion and not be afraid to ask for help.

Anna's journey shows us that a community is like a garden; it needs a girl who is willing to provide the water of a great idea and the nutrients of hard work. Through the broken pipes of her hydroponic system and the spicy kick of a fresh salsa snack, she cultivated a new understanding of health in her town. Anna reminds us that when we choose to grow healthy, we aren't just planting seeds in a wall; we are planting a future where every child has the knowledge to bloom into their best self.

Chapter 3
The Flavor of Home

Aanya Kasera (Ep 159)

The Secret Lunchbox

Aanya Kasera moved from the vibrant, spice-filled air of India to the snowy plains of Wisconsin, but the cold weather wasn't the only thing that felt different. As a young girl in a new country, she often felt like a puzzle piece forced into the wrong box. In the school cafeteria, while other kids unpacked sandwiches and chips, Aanya's lunchbox held the rich, aromatic scents of home. But instead of feeling proud, she felt a wave of anxiety. "I was scared to eat my Indian food in front of my friends," she remembered. She would sometimes choose to sit completely alone, hiding her meal so no one could judge the colors or the smells that were so dear to her family.

It wasn't just the food. Aanya loved Bharatanatyam, a traditional Indian classical dance filled with expressive storytelling and rhythmic footwork. To her, it was a beautiful way to connect with her roots, but to the outside world, she feared it would just be another thing that made her weird. She kept her passions tucked away like a secret, worried that if she shared the real Aanya, she wouldn't be accepted. This feeling of being alone in her cultural journey was heavy, like carrying an invisible backpack full of stones. She hadn't realized yet that many other kids felt the same way, including her own little sister.

Watching her sister go through those same struggles was the turning point. Her sister was also hesitant to bring friends home or share their Indian heritage. Aanya realized that if she didn't speak up, this cycle of hiding would just continue. She wanted to create a space where being different was celebrated, not feared. She decided to launch a project called Sharing the Joys of Cultural Diversity. Her goal was simple but powerful: she wanted to make sure no other kid felt like they had to hide their lunch or their dance just to fit in. By embracing her own story, she hoped to give others the courage to do the same.

From Scared to Storyteller

Aanya knew that a speech wouldn't be enough to change hearts: she needed a story. She decided the best way to reach younger children was through a picture book. She named her main character Saanvi and titled the book Samosas with Saanvi. The story followed Saanvi's journey from India to Wisconsin, mirroring Aanya's own experiences with cultural dresses, food, and the fear of being misunderstood. Aanya spent months drafting the narrative, ensuring that every anecdote felt real and relatable. She wanted kids to see themselves in Saanvi, whether they were from India, Mexico, or right there in the Midwest.

But writing the book was only half the plan. To make a real difference, she needed to get into classrooms and talk to her peers. She partnered with a teacher, Miss Emily Burnt, at a local school to work with a sixth-grade world studies class. Together, they looked at the curriculum and found a way to weave Aanya's message of diversity into their lessons. It wasn't just about Aanya talking; it was about the students researching and sharing, too.

To carry out this massive undertaking, Aanya followed a structured plan:

- She collaborated with her project advisor to integrate cultural discussions into the sixth-grade world studies curriculum.
- She designed and led interactive presentations for the students about the importance of researching different heritages.
- She utilized the local public library to host a community reading event for families and children.

Aanya's vision was to create a collaborative discussion space where culture could be talked about freely. She held group discussions and even met with students individually to hear their stories. It was a lot of work for a high school student, but seeing the excitement in the classroom made every hour worth it. She was no longer just a girl with a secret; she was an author and a leader on a mission.

The Formatting Fumble

The road to becoming a published author was bumpier than Aanya expected. While she had plenty of passion, she didn't have much experience with the technical side of bookmaking. "Writing a book is really a difficult process," she admitted, "something that I didn't fully think about when I was planning my project". After she finished the story and found a way to get illustrations, the real nightmare began: formatting for Amazon.

She had designed everything on a program called Canva, and it looked perfect on her computer screen. But when she tried to upload it to the publishing site, the layout completely broke. Pictures were in the wrong places, and the words didn't line up. "I was googling for hours on how to fix it," Aanya recalled. It was late in the process, and she started to panic. She worried that all her hard work would be stuck behind a computer glitch. But Aanya didn't give up. She stayed resilient, searching for solutions and tweaking the files until every page was exactly where it needed to be.

Beyond the computer screen, another challenge loomed: her own nerves. Even though she had grown a lot, sharing her personal story with the community was still scary. Being vulnerable and telling people about the times she felt ashamed of her culture wasn't easy. She had to overcome the lingering fear of judgment that had followed her since she first moved to America. However, she realized that her vulnerability was her greatest strength. By being honest about her struggles, she was making it safe for others to be honest about theirs. She learned that even if something small goes wrong, there is always a solution if you keep pushing.

A Classroom of Cultures

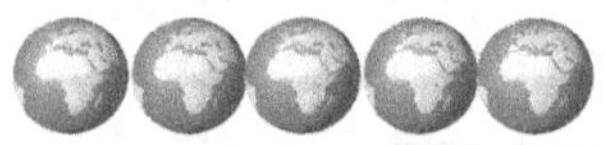

The impact of Aanya's project was visible in the eyes of the students she mentored. After weeks of presentations and research projects on cultures ranging from French to Chinese, the classroom felt different. The students weren't just learning facts from a textbook; they were learning about each other. Aanya sat in on their final presentations and was blown away by their collaboration and communication skills. "It was really meaningful to me just because it was another way to see how the project really impacted the students," she said.

One of the most touching moments came when a student approached Aanya to talk about her friend who wore a hijab to school. Before Aanya's lessons and the class research, the student didn't understand what the headscarf meant or why her friend wore it. But through the classroom discussions, she finally understood its cultural and religious significance. This understanding turned curiosity into respect, strengthening the bond between the two friends.

Another student shared that she had never really cared about her own heritage before. But after hearing Aanya's story and doing her own research, her mindset shifted. She told Aanya she wanted to go home and ask her parents questions about their ancestors and their background. Aanya was incredibly proud of this shift. Her project had succeeded in making students curious about the world and their own place in it. By the end of the term, "Diversity is with everyone" wasn't just a phrase; it was a reality students lived every day in their hallways.

Beyond the Final Page

Today, Aanya is a college student on a premed track, aiming for a future career in medicine. She attributes much of her success to the leadership skills she built through her project and her time in HOSA, a future health professional organization. Before all this, Aanya described herself as shy and someone who didn't like public speaking. But the project forced her to find her voice. Now, she's a confident leader who has traveled the world, from the mountains of Switzerland to an internship in Brazil.

Aanya's adventures didn't stop there. She still remembers the fun times she had with her friends, like a trip to a campsite where they stayed in a yurt. They spent the night bonding, telling spooky stories, and cooking for each other. Aanya even made a special sandwich with different vegetables and her own homemade sauce. These moments of sisterhood reminded her that while the work was important, the friendships made along the way were just as vital.

Looking toward the future, Aanya doesn't plan on putting her pen down. "I definitely do want to start publishing more books again," she shared, mentioning her interest in both children's books and novels. She wants to continue sharing her story and perhaps even branch out into fiction. Her advice to any young person with a big goal is not to shy away from it. Even if the goal seems impossible or too high, Aanya is proof that with passion and a supportive community, you can turn a secret into a story that changes the world. "Whatever you're passionate about," she encouraged, go for it.

Aanya's journey is like the Samosas with Saanvi she wrote about: a blend of different ingredients that, when brought together, create something rich and wonderful. Just like a spicy samosa needs both the dough and the filling to be complete,

Aanya learned that she needed both her Indian roots and her American experiences to be herself fully. Her project was the bridge that allowed her to cross from a place of fear into a world of confidence. Now, she stands as a beacon for other youth, reminding them that their unique flavor is exactly what the world needs.

Chapter 4
The Voice of Courage

Madison Garrett (Ep 79)

The Heavy Silence

Madison Garrett has always been a girl who pays close attention to the heartbeat of her community. Growing up in a world that often feels fast and loud, she noticed a particular kind of quiet settling over her neighborhood as the global pandemic took hold. It wasn't just the silence of empty streets or closed schools; it was the heavy, unspoken weight of mental health struggles within minority communities. Madison watched as her peers and elders grappled with a world that seemed to be turning upside down. The shift to remote learning was difficult enough, but it was coupled with the painful reality of racial injustice, highlighted by the tragic stories of George Floyd and Breonna Taylor.

Madison felt a deep, personal motivation to act. She realized that while everyone was talking about physical health and masks, very few in her community were discussing the mind. "In minority communities, mental health is such a stigma," she observed, noting that many people felt ashamed to admit they were struggling. She didn't want the people she loved to suffer in secret. She knew that to make a difference, she had to become an advocate who could speak in a culturally sensitive, empowering way. Her goal for her project was clear: she would take a stand and advocate for mental health within her community, helping to tear down the walls of stigma that had stood for generations.

She started by looking at the youngest members of her circle. She visited a group of girls and began to break down the complex idea of mental health into pieces they could understand. She taught them about the importance of self-esteem and showed them how to use breathing exercises when they get frustrated. For Madison, this wasn't just a project requirement; it was a mission to equip her community with the tools to survive a traumatic time. She believed that if she could start the conversation with the youth, the ripples would eventually reach the parents and the elders, creating a new culture of openness and care.

The Virtual Soapbox

Carrying out the project required Madison to become a master of digital communication. Since the world was locked down, she couldn't host a traditional town hall meeting or pass out flyers in person. Instead, she turned her laptop into a command center and used Zoom as her virtual soapbox. She spent hours researching the rising suicide rates among African American adolescents, a heartbreaking trend that she felt needed immediate attention. She didn't just keep this information to herself; she reached out to the New York Beacon, a local newspaper, and began writing articles that highlighted the trauma Black youth experience daily.

Madison knew that her voice alone might not be enough to convince everyone, so she focused on building a team of professionals to lend her message weight. She wasn't afraid to reach out to people in high positions, knowing that you can do anything you put your mind to. She coordinated with healthcare experts and government representatives to ensure her community received the best possible information. To keep the project moving forward during the height of the pandemic, she utilized several key partnerships and tools:

- **Professional Medical Insights**: She partnered with Dr. Audrey Sealey, a nurse practitioner, to provide clinical expertise during her mental health seminars.

- **Government Collaboration**: She worked with a representative of Eric Adams to give the topic of community wellness civic importance.

- **Journalistic Advocacy**: She leveraged her role as a writer for the New York Beacon to reach thousands of readers who might not have access to digital seminars.

- **Digital Connectivity:** She used Zoom and Google Meet as primary platforms to bring people from across the country together when they were physically isolated.

Through these actions, Madison transformed her individual passion into a community-wide resource. She was no longer just a high school student; she was a coordinator for a national conversation. She found that the project's virtual nature was an advantage, allowing her to reach a much broader audience than an in-person event in a single building could. Madison's project became a bridge, connecting isolated individuals with the expert care and sisterly support they so desperately needed.

Breaking Through Walls

Every leader faces a mountain to climb, and for Madison, that mountain was her junior year of high school. Academically, junior year is known for being one of the most rigorous and stressful times for any student. Madison was navigating it during a time when schools shut down. She had to manage her project while sitting at a screen for hours on end, attending classes on Google Meet, and keeping up with a demanding extracurricular schedule. She admitted that finishing her project during this time was a "pretty big challenge to say is an understatement".

The isolation of remote learning could have easily led to procrastination or a loss of focus. Madison had to find a way to stay self-motivated when she couldn't see her teammates or her mentors in person. She often felt pressure to doubt her own capabilities as a young woman in leadership. However, she didn't let these moments of doubt stop her. She leaned on her mother, stepfather, and grandparents, who provided the encouragement she needed to keep going. She also realized that being quiet is often the most important sign of a mental health crisis, and she used that knowledge to push through her own struggles.

Madison learned that being a leader doesn't mean having no fear; it means moving forward even when you are unsure. She had to re-evaluate her plans constantly as the pandemic evolved. While she was disappointed that she "wasn't able to serve bagels and coffee" or have the warmth of a physical gathering, she focused on the opportunity to bring people from across the country together. By the time she reached the final stages of her project, Madison had proven that her resilience was stronger than the walls of her own room. She had turned a time of global crisis into a period of intense personal growth, discovering that she had the power to manage complex logistics and emotional challenges simultaneously.

A Meeting Of Minds

The true impact of Madison's project became visible during the seminar she hosted. It was a rare moment where generations collided in a shared space of vulnerability. Madison watched as conversations during the event began to change the way people viewed themselves and their families. She was most proud of how the seminar enabled people of different ages to understand one another's pain. She heard teenagers speak about the hidden issues that come with remote learning, while parents admitted they didn't know what to do as they watched their children isolate themselves.

Perhaps the most touching part of the impact was Madison's interaction with the community elders. Many of the seniors who attended the seminar had never considered mental health as something that applied to them. They were from a generation taught to be strong and keep moving forward without complaint. However, Madison's seminar gave them the vocabulary to describe the anxiety they were feeling while stuck at home. By providing a safe space for these conversations to take place, Madison successfully began to destigmatize the topic of mental health.

Madison also shared a powerful takeaway that anyone can use to help their friends. She emphasized that "the quiet is usually the most important sign". She taught her audience that instead of minding your own business when a friend seems sad or isolated, you should ask if they are okay. This simple shift from distance to connection became the hallmark of her work. Madison's project didn't just provide information; it provided healing. She saw that the trauma of the past and the uncertainty of the present could be managed if people were willing to work toward a common goal of wellness.

Beyond The Sash

Madison's journey as a leader did not end with her project. In fact, it was just the beginning of a life dedicated to service and social justice. She serves as the president of the National Council of Negro Women, where she organizes Mother's Day brunches for women in domestic abuse shelters and superhero days for children in hospitals. She is also the founder and editor-in-chief of Gen Z's Voices. This magazine enables young people to raise awareness of the school-to-prison pipeline and other critical social justice issues. Madison believes that young voices matter, even in a world that often tries to silence them.

Looking ahead, Madison has set her sights on the highest levels of education and advocacy. She plans to study political science with interests in economics and neuroscience at Columbia University. She wants to continue her work in mental health by shooting a documentary that explores the effects of mental health during the slave times and during the civil rights movement. Whether she becomes a playwright, a lawyer who helps juveniles, or a politician who passes legislation, Madison is determined to make a difference for all. She is a girl who knows her passion and is not afraid to chase after it.

Madison's advice to other girls is to "never give up on yourself" and to "always believe in yourself". In the end, Madison learned that leadership is a lot like a lighthouse in a storm. The waves of the pandemic and the winds of injustice were strong, but by keeping her voice of courage shining, she guided her community toward a safer shore. Her project wasn't just a collection of seminars and articles; it was a permanent beam of light that reminded everyone, from the youngest child to the oldest elder, that they never have to navigate the darkness of their minds alone. Madison proved that when one girl decides to speak her truth, she gives thousands of others permission to find their own.

Chapter 5

A Boutique for Belonging

Sofia Martinez (Ep 134)

The Spark Behind the Hangers

Sofia Martinez grew up in Las Vegas, a city known for its bright lights and constant energy, but she was more interested in the stories that didn't make it onto the billboards. Her journey towards her Girl Scout Gold Award didn't start with a desire for a pin; it started at the dinner table. Sofia's mother was a dedicated social worker, and through her, Sofia caught glimpses of a world many of her peers never saw: foster care. She listened to stories about teenagers who were navigating the same difficult math tests and friendship drama as she was, but with one massive added weight: they didn't have a permanent place to call home.

As she brainstormed for her project, Sofia realized that foster youth faced a unique, invisible barrier when it came to major life milestones. While other students were buzzing about prom night or nervously preparing for their first job interviews, foster teens were often worrying about what they would wear. Some agencies provided clothing, but many required the teens to disclose their foster care status just to get a dress or a suit. Sofia thought about how hard it is to be a teenager even in the best circumstances. She knew that having to announce you were in foster care just to get a pair of shoes for an interview felt like a blow to your dignity.

"It's hard enough being a teenager, but being a teenager in foster care, that's not any easier," Sofia realized as she developed her mission. She envisioned a place that felt less like a charity donation center and more like a high-end clothing store. A boutique where a girl could find a stunning gown or a boy could find a crisp shirt for an interview without ever having to explain who they were or where they came from. This concept was the driving force behind her project, which she named Beyond the Attic Boutique. She wanted to create a safe space where foster youth could shop with their heads held high, focusing on their bright futures rather than their current labels.

The Power of Rerouting

Even with a heart full of passion, Sofia quickly discovered that leading a major project is rarely a straight path to success. Her first big plan was to partner with a club at her high school to place donation bins in the hallways. She figured it would be an easy way to collect clothes from her classmates and transport them to the local child haven. However, the school administration gave her a disappointing answer: "No." Because the school already had several other drives happening, they couldn't approve another one. This was a crushing moment for a freshman who had put so much effort into her vision.

Sofia admitted that facing rejection early on was incredibly difficult. She felt the sting of disappointment, wondering if her project would ever get off the ground if she couldn't even get support from her own school. But this is where Sofia learned one of the most important leadership lessons: "Rejection is redirection." She didn't let the no stop her; instead, she turned to her support system. Her mentor, Gretchen, guided Sofia through the roadblocks, showing her that there was always another way to reach a goal if you were willing to be flexible.

Gretchen helped Sofia see that her original vision wasn't the only vision that would work. Instead of relying on a school club, Sofia decided to work directly with the Department of Family Services and a local contact named Holly. Holly posted Sofia's flyers across the Las Vegas Valley, reaching an audience far beyond just one high school. Sofia also reached out to the president of her school's Key Club, who helped circulate her flyers even though they couldn't have the physical bins on campus. By learning to roll with the punches and seek secondary options, Sofia turned a major setback into a wider community connection. She realized that being a leader meant being patient with the process and trusting that a different road could still lead to the same beautiful destination.

The Boutique Blueprint

With her team in place and her flyers circulating, the physical work of creating Beyond the Attic Boutique began. Sofia wasn't just collecting clothes; she was designing an experience. She secured a space within Child Haven adjacent to a donation center called Peggy's Attic. To make the space special, she had to think about logistics, marketing, and interior design all at the same time. She realized that to get the high-quality items foster youth deserved, she couldn't just ask for old clothes; she had to ask for special occasion wear.

Sofia's strategy for carrying out the project relied on clear communication and specific organizational steps. She spent hours coordinating with her project advisor, Denise, who ran Peggy's Attic, to ensure the new boutique met the facility's needs. To keep the project organized and professional, she followed several key steps:

- Designed and distributed eye-catching flyers both in her school and across the local community to specify the need for formal and interview attire.

- Established a permanent partnership with the Department of Family Services to ensure that caseworkers knew the boutique was a resource for their teens.

- Developed an anonymous feedback system using paper forms so that she could measure the impact of the boutique while protecting the privacy of the shoppers.

The community's response was overwhelming and joyful to witness. People didn't just donate old items; they brought in high-quality pieces that made Sofia's eyes widen in surprise. She found herself sorting through dozens of beautiful pageant dresses from top brands like Sherri Hill, realizing that people were truly supporting her mission. On the official set-up day, a massive group of her friends and fellow students showed up at Child Haven to help her transform the space. Seeing so many people standing together for a group photo, surrounded by racks of colorful gowns and sharp suits, was one of Sofia's favorite memories. She had successfully turned a simple idea into a professional boutique, proving that when you provide a clear plan, the community will step up to help you build it.

Prom Dreams and Full Circles

The true measure of Sofia's project wasn't the number of dresses on the rack, but the smiles on the faces of the teens who wore them. Because foster youth are a vulnerable population, Sofia had to be careful about how she collected her data. She didn't want to intrude on their privacy, so she created an anonymous form for them to fill out after they shopped in the boutique. The results were more heartwarming than she could have ever anticipated.

One story stuck with Sofia and made all the hours of research and flyer-printing worth it. Her advisor, Denise, sent her a message about the very first girl who visited the boutique. The girl was looking for a prom dress, and when she stepped into the space Sofia had created, she found the perfect gown. She was so excited and relieved that she didn't have to worry about the cost or her foster status while preparing for her big night. Hearing that the project she had worked on for nearly two years had brought that kind of joy to a peer was a full-circle moment for Sofia.

The impact of Beyond the Attic Boutique extended beyond the physical clothes. By providing formal wear and interview attire, Sofia was giving foster youth the confidence to be themselves. She was helping them navigate the difficult transition into adulthood with dignity. The boutique remains an ongoing resource at Child Haven, with Holly from Family Services continuing to spread the word to donors every year to keep the racks replenished. Sofia realized that her project had achieved the goal: it was sustainable, it addressed a root cause of foster teen isolation, and it gave her a sense of fulfillment that changed the way she viewed her own power to make a difference. She had proven that a single girl with a vision could remove a barrier for hundreds of others, one prom dress at a time.

Boutique to the Bedside

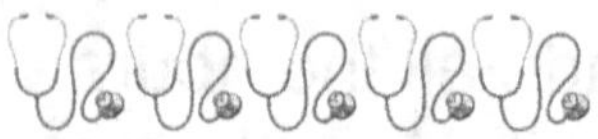

Completing this massive project changed Sofia from a nervous teenager into a confident leader. The skills she honed while navigating rejection and managing a community-wide drive carried over into the next chapter of her life. During her senior year, she had the incredible opportunity to serve as a delegate at the Girl Scout National Convention. Although the pandemic forced the event to move to Zoom, Sofia found the experience eye-opening. She got to speak with the governor of Pakistan and meet girls from across the globe, learning about their ways of life and seeing how girls everywhere advocate for what they believe in.

Sofia moved from Nevada to Alabama for college. She admitted that going somewhere where she knew nobody was scary, but the confidence she gained from her project gave her the foundation she needed to thrive in a new environment. She is majoring in nursing, with a future goal of earning her master's degree and becoming a nurse practitioner. Her desire to help people, sparked by her mother's social work and her own project, has now become her lifelong career path.

Sofia's advice to any girl starting her own mission is to remember that the hard stuff is worth it. She knows the hours will add up, and the roadblocks will be frustrating, but she promises that "the payoff is definitely worth it." Looking back, she sees that being a part of Girl Scouts for over twelve years wasn't just about selling cookies; it was about building a sisterhood and developing the ability to see a project through to the very end. Sofia's journey from the Las Vegas valley to the college campus is proof that a girl's voice is a powerful force for change.

Sofia's project is like the precise tailoring of a beautiful gown: she took the raw fabric of a community need, carefully cut away the jagged edges of rejection and stigma, and stitched together a permanent sanctuary of dignity that allows every foster teen to step into the spotlight of their own life, feeling perfectly fitted for success.

Chapter 6
Colors of Strength

Shay Roy-Lewis (Ep 157)

The Quiet Canvas

Shay Roy-Lewis grew up in the heart of Madison, Wisconsin, surrounded by a world that was constantly buzzing with noise. But for Shay, the most important conversations were often the ones that happened in silence, through the strokes of a paintbrush or the texture of a collage. As a girl who had been part of her local troop for eleven years, she had seen many friends struggle with the weight of being a teenager. She noticed that whenever people talked about mental health for girls her age, the conversation was almost always heavy and negative. It felt like a dark cloud that everyone acknowledged, but no one knew how to paint with bright colors. Shay knew she wanted to change that. She wanted to showcase the strength and power of young women.

Shay wasn't just a casual observer; she was an artist herself. Art had been her passion since before she could even remember, and she understood that images could sometimes say what words could not. She dreamed of creating a space where girls in Madison and Dane County could share their stories of resilience, culture, and identity through the fine arts. She envisioned an exhibition that wouldn't just focus on the struggle, but on the incredible power found within it. She wanted to shift the conversation from sadness to celebration. This personal motivation was the fuel for her upcoming project, but she knew that to make it a reality, she would have to step out from behind her own canvas and lead.

As she began to plan, the scale of the idea felt massive. She wasn't just looking for a school hallway to hang pictures; she wanted a professional stage. She set her sights on the Overture Center for the Arts, a premier performing arts center that hosts Broadway musicals and world-class orchestras. It is a place of high ceilings and large windows, a hub for performing arts and fine arts right in the middle of downtown. To a high school student, the idea of approaching such a prestigious institution felt beyond her reach. She felt the flutter of nerves every time she thought about it, but she remembered the many years she had spent volunteering at food pantries and the Ronald McDonald House with her troop. Those experiences had taught her that taking the first step to help others was always worth the fear.

The Courage To Click Send

The transition from dreaming to doing required a different kind of bravery. Shay had to navigate the professional world of museum curators and gallery directors, a world she was completely unfamiliar with at the start. She began by sending out random emails to local museum professionals, hoping someone would see the value in her vision. It was a period of waiting and wondering, a test of her confidence. She realized that she couldn't afford to be afraid of the word "no" if she wanted to hear a "yes." She had to believe that her message was important enough for others to listen. This part of the project taught her a vital lesson: you never know how people will respond until you try.

One of those blind emails landed in Jody Klaus's inbox, the director of the James Watrous Gallery. Jody proved to be a huge support for Shay. She saw the spark in the young artist's proposal and didn't just offer advice; she opened doors. Jody connected Shay with the staff at the Overture Center, who were overwhelmingly supportive of the goal to highlight teen girls' mental health. Suddenly, the big undertaking began to feel possible. Shay was no longer just a girl with an idea; she was the curator of an upcoming exhibition in the Rotunda Gallery, a space with large windows facing State Street that guaranteed a lot of foot traffic.

Working with professionals was a major revelation for Shay. She learned that businesses and large organizations have people who are often just as passionate about community as she was. By stepping into this professional environment, she had to learn the logistics and language of the art world. She had to stay organized, manage multiple deadlines, and communicate clearly with the Overture staff. She couldn't let anything slip, or she believed she would be letting people down. Her growth as a leader unfolded in real time as she balanced the gallery's needs with her vision for the artists.

The Jury and the Catalog

With the gallery space secured, Shay launched an open call for submissions. She used a program called Airtable to collect applications from young women across high schools in the area. Soon, she was looking at a digital gallery of incredible talent. To ensure the show was of the highest quality, she formed a jury. This team consisted of herself, her advisor Jody, museum coordinator Megan Landon, and the Overture Galleries director, Stephanie Barenz. They met over a Zoom call to review every piece of art, using a rating scale to rate each work and discussing how each would fit into the show's overall theme. Shay had to lead these discussions, ensuring the artists' visions and intentions were at the forefront of the selection process.

Managing sixteen different artists was a logistical puzzle that required constant attention. Each artist had a unique voice and a unique story to tell through topics like culture and sexual identity. Shay had to coordinate several rounds of materials from each of them, checking her email multiple times a day to keep track of every moving part. She was the bridge between the professional standards of the Overture Center and the raw, creative energy of the high school artists. She had to ensure that every artist felt supported while also meeting the gallery's strict requirements.

To make the project truly professional, Shay went beyond just hanging art on a wall. She focused on several key tools to make the impact last:

- **Airtable**: Used to create a structured open call and jury rating system for submissions.

- **Canva**: Allowed her to design a professional Instagram presence and exhibition catalog.

- **Amazon Publishing**: She created an exhibition catalog listing every piece and its artist statement, making it available for public purchase even after the show closed.

By creating the catalog, Shay ensured that the voices of these sixteen young women wouldn't disappear when the gallery's lights went out. She also built a website that linked the artists to their own professional pages.

Hard Choices

Being a leader meant Shay had to handle the part of the job that no one likes, rejection. Because the gallery space was limited, she couldn't accept everyone who applied. Sending out acceptance and denial emails was the most difficult part for her because she never wanted to say no to anyone.

She realized that when you are working on the whole project, you sometimes make sacrifices that aren't fun. It was an emotional challenge that required her to be professional and firm, even when it was difficult. She had to trust that the sixteen artists she did select would carry out their personal visions in a way that would make the entire show cohesive.

The technical side of the gallery also presented hurdles. The Rotunda Gallery space best displays 2D media, such as paintings and collages. However, one artist submitted a 3D sculpture piece. Shay and the museum staff had to find a way to present it on the wall space to include this more dimensional experience for visitors, requiring creative problem-solving to work within the gallery's constraints. Shay's ability to navigate these technicalities showed how much her leadership skills had evolved from the start of the project.

The stakes grew even higher when the local news caught wind of the exhibition. On the day of the opening, Channel 3000 came to the gallery to do a live television interview with Shay. Standing in front of a camera and speaking to the entire city was an amazing experience that tested her public speaking skills. She had to represent not just herself, but the sixteen artists and the message of mental health awareness she had worked so hard to promote. It was a proud moment that showed she had found the confidence and public-speaking ability she once doubted she had.

Guest Book Glow

The Her Art exhibition ran for two months, from September to November 2024. The Rotunda Gallery was constantly packed with people who had stopped to look through the large windows or who had come specifically for the show. The energy in the room during the reception was incredible, as artists brought their families and friends to see their work in a professional setting. Shay watched as people moved from piece to piece, reading the artist statements and reflecting on the unique works that demonstrated each girl's personal experience. The show was a massive success, but the true measure of its impact was found in a small book at the entrance.

Shay had placed a gallery guest book by the front of the exhibition for visitors to write their thoughts and feelings. When she went through it for the first time, she was overwhelmed and so happy to see the messages people had left. The feedback confirmed that her project had reached people's hearts. One visitor wrote about how much the art had touched them, while others expressed how empowered they felt by seeing the strength of young women on display. Reading those messages was an incredible moment for Shay, proving that she had successfully brought light to a topic that was often kept in the dark.

Shay's growth as a leader extended far beyond Madison. As a world traveler who had visited Paris and Spain and was preparing for a hike to Machu Picchu in Peru, she saw her project as part of a global perspective. She understood that seeing how other people lived was a valuable experience she wanted to bring back into her art. Now, as she looks toward a future in character art, animation, or art history, she carries with her the lessons of the Rotunda Gallery. She knows that even if a goal seems big and out of your reach, the best thing you can do is your best and trust the process.

Shay's journey is much like the gallery itself, a space filled with different perspectives that, when brought together, create a masterpiece. Her project was the frame that held these diverse stories in place, allowing the community to see the vibrant colors of strength within every girl. Just as a curator must choose which pieces to highlight to tell a complete story, Shay learned to choose courage over fear and action over silence. Now, the catalog of her experience serves as a permanent record that when you combine passion with leadership, you can paint a future where every voice is seen, every story is heard, and every girl knows she has the power to change the world.

Chapter 7
Class of Kindness

Jola Stayhorn (Ep 158)

Silence After the Storm

Jola Stayhorn was always a girl on the move. As a standout sprinter at Union Catholic High School, she was used to the explosive energy of the track, the sound of the starting gun, and the wind rushing past her ears as she flew toward the finish line. She competed in everything from the 55-meter dash to the 400-meter dash, thriving on the pumped-up energy of huge national meets in places like Boston. But when the world slowed down during the pandemic, Jola noticed a different kind of silence, one that wasn't on the track, but in the hallways of elementary schools.

While the rest of the world was figuring out how to go back to normal, Jola looked at the youngest students, the kindergarteners, and realized they were struggling. These kids had spent a huge portion of their early lives at home, away from other children. When they finally stepped into a real classroom, they didn't know the unwritten rules of school. Jola saw that they had lost basic social skills, like walking in a straight line, raising their hands, and being quiet when a teacher was talking. "They should be free and just be able to be themselves and run around," Jola thought, but instead, she saw that "social anxiety was increasing more for the younger kids". They didn't even know how to share toys at recess.

Because Jola was deeply passionate about helping children and had already dreamed of becoming a social worker, she knew she had to act. She wanted to create something that would bridge the gap between their isolated years at home and their new lives in school. She decided her project would be a high-quality educational video designed specifically for kindergarteners. It wouldn't just be a lecture; it would be a fun, visual guide to help them feel confident in school. Jola knew that if she could help them master these simple interactions, their anxiety would fade, and they could get back to the joy of being a kid.

Paperwork Marathon

Even though Jola was a sprinter who liked things to happen quickly, she quickly learned that her project was more like a long-distance marathon. Before she could ever pick up a camera, she had to navigate a mountain of administrative hurdles. She hadn't expected this side of the process. Every time she submitted her plans or answered questions online, they seemed to come back with more requests for detail. "I was like, when am I finally going to get my project approved?" she remembered feeling.

The review committee kept sending her paperwork back for corrections. They wanted more details on why she chose the topic and exactly how she would measure the impact of her video. For a girl used to crossing finish lines in seconds, this waiting and revising was incredibly frustrating. It felt like every time she got close to the goal, the finish line was moved back another ten meters. She had to answer dozens of questions and justify every single piece of her plan.

Through this hard road, Jola discovered a level of patience she didn't know she had. She realized that the corrections weren't there to stop her, but to make her project better and more sustainable. She had to trust in God and keep her head down, even when the paperwork felt overwhelming. She told herself to keep "pushing forward to meet my goal at the end". This mental toughness, the same kind she used to stay focused during a high-stakes track meet with cameras everywhere, became her secret weapon. She learned that believing in herself was just as important as the project's actual work.

Lights, Camera, Action

Once the plans were finally approved, it was time to move into production. Jola didn't want the video to be her talking to the camera; she wanted it to feature kids whom the kindergarteners could relate to. She recruited a family friend's nieces to be the stars of the show. These little girls were roughly the same age as the audience, making the lessons feel more like a game than a classroom rulebook. Jola spent hours directing them, showing them how to demonstrate simple things like walking in a line and sharing.

Execution required a mix of creativity and technical problem-solving. To carry out her vision, Jola followed a very specific set of steps:

- She cast her family friend's nieces to act out the classroom scenarios to make the content relatable.

- She attempted to use the app CapCut to edit the footage, focusing on sound and lighting quality.

- She partnered with a friend, an experienced editor, to finalize the video when the technical side became too difficult.

The filming process brought its own set of surprises. Jola found out that making a video look good is much harder than it looks on social media. She struggled with the lighting and the sound, realizing that "making sure the sound and the lighting and all that... was very difficult". When her own attempts at editing on CapCut just weren't working, she showed great leadership by reaching out for help. She didn't let her ego get in the way; she called a friend who specialized in editing and asked for support to ensure the final product was the best it could be. By building a team, she ensured her project met the high standards she had set for herself.

New York Spotlight

When the video was finished, the impact was immediate and powerful. Jola went to a local school to premiere her work for a class of kindergarteners. As the video played, she watched as their faces lit up. The kids weren't just watching; they were learning. They had dozens of questions for Jola about how she filmed it and how they could be like the kids in the video. The teacher was incredibly appreciative because the video provided a tool that helped the entire class run more smoothly.

But the impact didn't stop there. Because Jola was a media girl for her council, she already had experience speaking in front of people and being on camera. Her project caught the attention of CBS in New York, and they invited her for a national interview, a huge, nerve-wracking opportunity. She had only two days to prepare, including a quick Zoom meeting on a Friday to prep for a Monday morning film shoot.

Jola traveled to New York, where she met the CEO of GSUSA. They bonded behind the scenes, talking about how they both loved to run track. When the cameras started rolling, Jola talked for twenty minutes about the importance of social skills and her passion for children. Even though the final clip was edited down to just two minutes, she had shared her message with a massive audience. This experience was amazing, teaching her that when you do something you love, you find the confidence to speak up even on the biggest stages.

Sprinter's Mindset

Completing the project changed how Jola saw herself as a leader. She realized that the skills she learned on the track: discipline, focus, and resilience, were the same skills she needed to change her community. "If you do a project that you hate doing and you're not even passionate about, why even do it?" she asked. She learned that picking a topic she truly cared about made the ups and downs worth the effort.

Jola's leadership growth was evident in her new roles at school, where she continued to serve as a mentor and a media girl, practicing the skill of expressing her personality and sharing her passions. She is now looking toward a future where she can continue this work on a larger scale. She plans to attend a D1 or D2 college on a track scholarship and major in social work so she can spend her life advocating for those who need a voice.

Her journey taught her that even the most challenging goals are reachable if you take them one step at a time. Whether she is running a 400-

meter relay or filling out a stack of paperwork, she knows that patience and perseverance are the keys to victory. Jola wants other girls to know that they should keep pushing forward and pick a topic that makes them feel carefree because passion makes hard work feel like joy.

Jola's story is a testament to the power of transformation through persistence. Like an athlete preparing for a championship race, she understood that the real work happened long before the cameras rolled or the final product was shared. The pressure she faced, endless revisions, technical hurdles, and the nerves of a national interview, did not slow her down; instead, those challenges sharpened her resolve and refined her purpose. Now, she moves toward her future like a sprinter out of the blocks: head up, eyes on the prize, and ready to win for herself and her community.

Chapter 8
1% Awareness Mission

Isabel Rosario (Ep 120)

The Forgotten Diagnosis

For Isabel Rosario, life shifted in an instant during October of 2019. It began with a phone call that no family ever wants to receive: her beloved grandfather had been diagnosed with breast cancer. To most people, the news was a double shock. Dealing with a cancer diagnosis is heavy enough for any family, but the Rosario family was stunned by a detail they never knew was possible. Like many others in their community, they simply did not know that men could even get breast cancer. Isabel quickly realized that her family's confusion wasn't an isolated incident; it was a symptom of a much larger, global lack of awareness.

Determined to understand what her grandfather was facing, Isabel dove into research. What she found was startling. While most breast cancer campaigns across the world are directed exclusively toward women, men make up approximately 1% of all cancer diagnoses. To some, one percent might seem like a tiny, insignificant number, but Isabel saw the faces behind the data. "1% is thousands of lives because of how many breast cancer diagnoses there are every year," she noted. Because the public doesn't talk about male breast cancer, men are often diagnosed at much later, more dangerous stages.

They don't know what symptoms to look for, and they don't have a community where they feel they belong.

Isabel watched as her grandfather struggled with this reality. He stayed quiet for several months because he didn't feel he could find anyone who related to his experience. There were no brochures for him, no support groups that felt welcoming, and a mountain of stereotypes that suggested he shouldn't have this female disease. Isabel realized that there was a lack of education and support for patients and their families; she was the one who had to start tackling it. She wanted to ensure that no matter a person's sex, they would feel empowered to go to the doctor for checkups if they noticed unusual symptoms. This spark led to the creation of her project, titled "The 1%: A Human Race Breast Cancer Awareness".

Breaking Through The Stigma

As Isabel began her project, she quickly discovered that the biggest obstacle wasn't the biology of the disease, but the silence of the culture surrounding it. There is a profound stigma associated with men having breast cancer, often rooted in outdated ideas of what it means to be manly. Isabel interviewed other survivors to build a platform where their voices could finally be heard. One story left her completely shocked. She interviewed a man whose own father refused to speak to him for seven years after his diagnosis because the father believed having breast cancer meant his son wasn't manly enough.

Isabel found this heartbreaking because she knew that when someone is fighting for their life, family support is one of the most vital tools for recovery. These stereotypes were literally stopping people from getting the help and love they needed to survive. She wanted to change the narrative and let every man know that it is okay to have this diagnosis. "Men have breasts too," she emphasized, "and it is not the person's fault". She realized that her mission had to be about more than just facts and figures; it had to be about changing hearts and minds so that optimism and positivity could replace shame and isolation.

The sensitivity of the topic required Isabel to be incredibly careful with her words. When she shared her grandfather's story on social media, she would always send him the post and the photo first to make sure he was comfortable with the message. She tackled difficult subjects like alopecia, which can be very sensitive for patients losing their hair during treatment. She also made sure to show that while optimism is important, it is also okay for patients to be sad, frustrated, or to cry. By being authentic and showing another side of the illness, she began to build a bridge of trust with survivors who had been hiding in the shadows for years.

A Law For The People

Isabel was not satisfied with just making a website or giving a few speeches. She wanted to create a permanent, systemic change that would last forever in her home of Puerto Rico. She decided that the island needed a dedicated day to highlight the 1% that is often forgotten. Her goal was to declare the second Friday of October as Male Breast Cancer Awareness Day. This was an incredibly ambitious goal for a high school student, requiring her to navigate the complex world of government and legislation.

The process was a grueling journey that took nine months of persistence and patience. Isabel learned that the government moves slowly, and she had to be the one to keep pushing. She spent months emailing and calling representatives, only to find that they wouldn't answer. When she couldn't find a public email address for a specific official, she would research the organization's standard email format and guess the official's address based on their name, hoping the message would land. This outside-the-box thinking eventually paid off when she was called into the office of the Senate President of Puerto Rico.

To carry out this massive legislative project, Isabel managed several high-stakes steps that required her to act as a professional advocate:

- Proposed the bill to the Senate President, explaining the data behind male breast cancer and the need for early detection.

- Testified before the House of Representatives, answering questions from lawmakers about the impact of the law on public health.

- Collaborated with the Governor's office to ensure the Senate bill was officially signed into law as Law 15-201.

- Partnered with global organizations like Susan G. Komen and the American Cancer Society to promote the new awareness day through Facebook Live events and speeches.

The day the governor signed the bill at La Fortaleza, the governor's house, was a moment Isabel will never forget. She stood there with her parents and her grandparents, watching as her grandfather's struggle was transformed into a law that would save lives for generations to come. This experience taught her that the person who wants the change the most must be the one to go for it. She realized that she wasn't just a girl with a project; she was a leader who had used her voice to create a legacy of protection for every man on her island.

Leading Through Lockdown

Just as Isabel was starting to develop the main components of her mission, the world was hit by the 2020 pandemic. It was a terrifying time for her family, especially since her grandfather's life-saving surgery happened just days before everything shut down. Because of the lockdown, Isabel could no longer give in-person speeches or host community events. This was a major challenge, but she refused to let the pandemic silence her message. She decided to use the power of social media to reach her audience.

Isabel used her time in virtual school to become a master of time management. While other students might have spent their 10-minute breaks between Zoom classes scrolling through aimless videos, Isabel used those brief windows to work on her project. She would hop from one Zoom class to another and then spend an hour after her schoolwork was finished editing videos, writing captions, and interviewing survivors remotely. She recorded speeches on video and sent them to organizations for online sharing. She even hosted Facebook Live sessions to answer community questions.

The digital shift allowed her project to grow even larger than she originally planned. Through Instagram and Facebook, she connected with people far beyond Puerto Rico, reaching a global audience. She learned that even though the pandemic had brought challenges, it also brought new ways to be resilient. She didn't just adapt to the situation; she thrived in it, proving that a girl's passion for her mission is stronger than any travel block or social distancing rule. Her project became a lifelong project that she has continued for years, long after the official requirements were met.

Crown of Opportunities

Isabel's growth as a leader during her project opened doors she never could have imagined. Because of the connections she made through her work, she was selected for the G-Team, a group of 25 girls from the United States, Italy, Mexico, and Puerto Rico who helped plan the Girl Scout National Convention. This experience forced her to become even more independent, as she traveled to Orlando by herself for meetings, the first time she had ever flown alone. Being surrounded by other ambitious, outspoken girls pushed her to think even further outside the box.

One of the most breathtaking moments of her journey occurred when she was chosen as one of six girls to interview Michelle Obama. Isabel was so nervous that she was shaking the entire time, but the former First Lady made the environment feel safe and friendly. Isabel learned about the concept of becoming, that we never stop growing, learning, and changing. This lesson stayed with her as she transitioned to college at The Ohio State University, where she double majored in Communications and Environmental Policy. She plans to become an advocate for environmental and social issues, using the media and public-speaking skills she developed during her project to save the planet.

Isabel's journey from a girl shocked by a diagnosis to a national scholarship recipient is a testament to the power of perseverance. She proved that no problem is too small and no goal is too big if you have the drive to pursue it. Today, she continues to receive messages from people all over the world whose lives her work has impacted. Her grandfather is always so happy to hear about her latest gig or success, knowing that something truly good came out of his difficult diagnosis. Isabel's message to every girl is simple: "Give in to that thing in your brain telling you to make a difference. Just do it".

Isabel's project is like a lighthouse built on a rocky, fog-covered coastline: she took the dark, confusing statistics of a forgotten 1% and used her voice to ignite a brilliant beam of awareness that now cuts through the clouds of stigma, ensuring that no man ever has to navigate the storm of a cancer diagnosis alone or in the dark.

Chapter 9
Sensory Friendly Futures

Lia Fasano (Ep 163)

The World Through Lia's Eyes

Lia Fasano was just two years old when she was diagnosed with autism, which meant she experienced the world a little differently than everyone else. For Lia, the sights, sounds, and textures of everyday life could sometimes feel like a radio turned up far too loud. As she grew up, she noticed a troubling gap in her community: there simply weren't enough sensory-friendly spaces where people like her could feel comfortable and regulated. While other kids might not think twice about the hum of a fluorescent light or the rough fabric of a chair, Lia knew that for neurodivergent people, these small things could be overwhelming.

Even at the young age of ten, Lia began to carry a dream in her heart. She didn't just want to fit into the world; she wanted to change it. She wanted to create something that would show people what it was like to live from her perspective and, more importantly, how neurodivergent people cope with the world around them. She wanted to spark a conversation about neurodiversity, the idea that all brains work differently and that those differences are something to be respected, not fixed.

As a girl who had spent years navigating these challenges, Lia decided her project would be the perfect way to turn her personal experience into a public resource. She called it Sensory Friendly

Futures. Her goal was to raise awareness by creating specialized fidget bins for public areas such as libraries and schools. This wasn't just a school assignment for Lia; it was her main passion. She wanted to bridge the gap between those who understood autism and those who didn't, using tactile tools to create a more inclusive community for everyone.

Science of a Fidget

Lia knew that a fidget wasn't just a toy; it was a tool for regulation and focus. She spent a great deal of time carefully selecting items for her 20 fidget bins to ensure they provided the right kind of sensory input. She wanted a variety of textures, smooth, spiky, squishy, to help people calm down when the world felt too loud. She even worked with her advisor to design a special logo for the lids so the bins would be easily recognizable.

Inside each bin, Lia packed a treasure trove of sensory tools. She included calming strips with a unique texture for people to touch when they needed to ground themselves. There were water timers that were mesmerizing to watch and pop tubes that made a satisfying sound when pulled apart and snapped back together. She also found a slug and a snake that moved in fun ways, which quickly became favorites among the people who used them.

To make her project professional, Lia reached out to actual companies for support. She was thrilled when brands like Crazy Aaron's Thinking Putty stepped up to help, donating dozens of tins of putty, including a Moonlight version that was holographic and others that changed color in the sun. Another sponsor, Little Ouchies, provided hand-sized rollers with tiny spikes that gave a great deal of sensory input. Lia even included homemade worry stones that her aunt, a pottery business owner, helped her create. Lia loved these items so much that she often kept a few in her own pencil case to help her get through class, and she knew they would help others just as much.

Pre-Law Professional

Bringing Sensory Friendly Futures to the public required Lia to act more like a lawyer than a high school student. She realized that for her project to be sustainable, meaning it would last for a long time, she needed a formal agreement with the places that hosted her bins. She drafted a two-page legal document that was so detailed and professional that people began telling her they could tell she was a pre-law student. She used logistical language to ensure everyone knew exactly how to care for the sensory tools.

Executing a plan of this size involved many moving parts and high-level coordination. To carry out her vision, Lia focused on these essential steps:

- She researched and drafted a two-page formal agreement to ensure the long-term maintenance of her fidget bins.

- She secured partnerships with the Valley Cottage Library, the Virtual School, and a local sensory room.

- She collaborated with her advisor, Allison, to manage communications and design professional labels for the bins.

Lia faced significant pushback on her agreement, especially over a line stating she could take the bins back if the rules weren't followed. Some organizations were scared by how serious she was, but Lia stood her ground. She knew that if the bins weren't maintained, they wouldn't help the kids who needed them most. She even had to make the tough decision to walk away from a large state-run hospital because the red tape and licensing requirements were too complex for her to handle at the time. She learned that part of leadership is knowing when to pivot and focus on partners who are truly ready to work with you.

Ugly Crying and Real Impact

The true test of Lia's project came when she started showcasing her bins at community events like Girl Scouts Love State Parks and Girlfest. She watched as people of all ages flocked to her table, drawn in by the colorful fidgets and the slug that made funny noises. In the feedback forms people filled out, almost everyone said the fidgets were their favorite part of the entire event. Lia had successfully turned her passion into a big hit that everyone could enjoy.

One memory stands out as the most special of all. At a state park event, a family approached Lia's booth. The mother looked at the bins and then at Lia, explaining that her own daughter was autistic. She told Lia how amazing it was to see someone raising awareness and fighting the stigma that often surrounds neurodivergent people. Lia was so moved by the mother's words and the connection they shared that she started crying right then and there.

It was in that moment that Lia realized the 80-plus hours of work she had put in were about more than just bins and putty. She had created a sense of community. She had made a mother feel seen, and a young girl feel supported. Lia's project had reached four different locations, including a school where she had a personal connection with the principal. By the time she received her final approval paperwork, Lia felt like she had achieved something that would stay with her for life.

Limitless Leader

Lia's journey didn't just change her community; it changed her. Before starting her project, Lia struggled with social anxiety so intense that she often didn't want to hang out with anyone or even talk to her teachers. But leading a large project forced her to find her voice. She had to learn how to public speak, write professional emails, and broaden her horizons through new connections. She realized that communication was the absolute key to everything, and she developed a limited tolerance for people who didn't respond to her emails in a timely manner.

Lia became the Vice President of Recruitment for a club at her school, a role where she actively goes out and talks to people to get them to join her team. She is no longer the shy girl who wanted to hide; she is a leader who knows how to build a team and advocate for a cause. She is pursuing her goal of becoming a lawyer and continues to mentor other girls who are working on their own high-level projects. She tells everyone she meets that the sky's the limit and encourages them to never listen to the negative thoughts in their heads.

Lia's advice to others is to start as early as possible and work closely with a mentor. She believes that if she could overcome her challenges, anyone can. "It's all mental," she says, reminding others that they are seen and loved. Lia Fasano took the radio of her world and found a way to tune it so that everyone, neurodivergent or not, could hear the music.

Lia learned to accept every challenge and turn it into an opportunity for growth. Her fidget bins are like anchors in a stormy sea, providing a steady place to hold on when life feels overwhelming. Now, as she moves toward a future in law, Lia serves as a reminder that when you follow your heart and trust your own point of view, you can build a future that is friendly for everyone.

Chapter 10

Whatever the Obstacle

Margaret Anne Mary Moore (Ep 129)

The Spark Of Normalcy

For Margaret Anne Mary Moore, growing up in Connecticut didn't feel like a series of limitations. It felt like a series of adventures. Margaret was born with cerebral palsy, a physical disability that meant she used a motorized wheelchair, a walker, and a specialized communication device to interact with the world. To many outsiders, these tools might have looked like barriers, but in Margaret's house, they were just part of the furniture of a very active life. Her mother, Anne, and her older brothers, Sean and Brian, never treated her as someone who needed to sit on the sidelines. They saw a girl who could play, laugh, and learn just like everyone else.

The family's strength was rooted in a legacy of resilience. Just before Margaret turned two, the family lost her father to stomach cancer. Despite the tragedy, her mother raised the three children with a powerful motto passed down from their father: "Whatever the obstacle, we will overcome it". Because of this unwavering support, Margaret was able to pursue a regular education, play sports, and join a Girl Scout troop where she could build her leadership skills. For a long time, Margaret assumed this was the standard experience for everyone with a disability. She thought all kids with physical challenges had the same green light to chase their dreams.

It wasn't until she was about eleven years old that the reality of the outside world began to sink in. People started telling her that her life was quite unusual. Most individuals with physical challenges didn't usually get to do everything Margaret was doing. She realized that many people were held back by a lack of support or by others' low expectations. This realization was a spark for her. She had already earned several honors in Girl Scouts, and she knew she wanted to tackle a project that would change these perceptions. She wanted to show the world that having a disability didn't mean having a lack of ambition. She decided to call her mission the Yes You Can Movement. Her goal was to motivate people of all abilities to look past their obstacles and reach for their greatest dreams.

Wall Of No

Even a girl as determined as Margaret eventually ran into a wall. As she began the prerequisites for her Gold Award, she encountered a hurdle she couldn't simply drive her wheelchair over. A leader who was supposed to be helping her troop told Margaret directly that she couldn't earn the Gold Award. The reason given was heartbreaking: "That's not something that kids with disabilities do". For the first time, Margaret was facing the very stereotypes she wanted to fight, and they were coming from someone within her own community. This rejection didn't just hurt her feelings; it delayed the start of her project for nearly a year.

However, Margaret was not a girl who gave up easily. She remembered her father's motto and leaned on her support system. While she felt the sting of the stereotype, she also knew she was more than what this one person believed. She attended a leadership camp called Camp CEO, where she met powerful women who saw her potential immediately. Mary Barnaby, the CEO of her council, and Teresa Younger, a board president and leader of the Ms. Foundation for Women, took her under their wing. These mentors didn't see a disability; they saw a leader with a vision. They pointed her in the right direction and encouraged her to keep moving forward despite the delay.

Finding these allies was a turning point. They provided the network that Margaret needed to back her project. Margaret realized that while some people would always try to define her by her physical limitations, many others were willing to help her succeed. Her mom continued to be her biggest cheerleader, and her brothers and school friends stepped up to participate in her plans. The discouragement she faced only made her more passionate about the Yes You Can Movement. It proved exactly why her project was necessary: she needed to make sure no other girl was told her dreams were off-limits because of a disability.

Blueprints Of Ambition

With a team of supporters behind her, Margaret began the detailed work of building the Yes You Can Movement. She wanted her project to be more than just a speech; she wanted it to be an experience that changed the way people thought. She spent hours planning a school-wide assembly and a keynote presentation for a major leadership conference at Salve Regina University. She worked with technical consultants and the professional motivational speaker Tracy Knofla to polish her delivery. Tracy even conducted a special coaching session with Margaret to ensure her presentations would have the greatest possible impact.

Margaret's execution of the project was thorough and creative. She didn't just want to tell her own story; she wanted to include her peers' voices as well. She grabbed a camera and started interviewing other high school students and alumni to find out what held them back from their ambitions. She also wanted people to think about the global consequences of giving up on a dream. She prepared a slideshow of famous people, like the founder of her own organization, Juliette Gordon Low, and asked the audience what the world would miss if those people hadn't followed their hearts.

To carry out the Yes You Can Movement, Margaret followed a specific set of actions:

- She interviewed students and alums about their obstacles and created an action-plan video to help them achieve their goals.

- She designed an interactive slide show featuring historical figures to illustrate the impact of personal ambition on the world.

- She developed a pre-presentation and post-presentation survey to measure whether her message improved the audience's outlook.

The logistics were intense, especially coordinating with the conference tech team for her projection and communication needs. But seeing the pieces come together was exciting. Margaret was creating a movement that used her own life story as proof that success was possible. She shared her experiences in school, sports, and leadership to show that stereotypes needed to be broken. She wanted every person in that room, whether they had a disability or not, to leave believing that they had something valuable to offer the world.

Voice Heard Round The Room

The day of the big presentation at the Salve Regina Leadership Conference finally arrived. Margaret sat before a room filled with 300 girls, ready to share her message. She could feel the support from her network in the audience; her mentor, Elizabeth Roth, was there, and Tracy Knofla had even surprised her by driving out to see her present. Using her communication device and her slides, Margaret led the audience through the Yes You Can journey. She asked them to consider their own dreams and what the world might miss out on if they let obstacles stand in their way.

The impact was visible immediately. As Margaret looked out at the sea of faces, she saw the positive outlook she had hoped to inspire. The surveys she handed out proved it: there was a measurable increase in how the attendees felt about their ability to reach their dreams after hearing her speak. Her project had reached its goal of boosting confidence and shifting mindsets. But Margaret didn't stop there. To make the project sustainable, she uploaded her presentation videos to YouTube and started a Facebook blog to post motivational messages.

This experience taught Margaret that her platform was just the beginning. She earned her Gold Award just before high school graduation in 2015, but she saw it as a launching point rather than a finish line. She realized that the skills she developed, public speaking, leadership, and organization, were tools she could use for the rest of her life. She had turned a moment of rejection from a troop leader into a successful movement that was now reaching people across the internet.

Margaret had found her voice, and she was determined to keep using it to advocate for a more accepting and compassionate world.

Marathon Of Success

After high school, Margaret brought the Yes You Can Movement's mission to Fairfield University, founding a club called Project Yes You Can and serving as its president for 4 years. The club grew to over 200 members and was named Club of the Year for its incredible service work, including serving at homeless shelters and organizing 5Ks for cancer research. Margaret also launched Positivity for Patients, where she partners with artists to donate motivational artwork to hospitals and lift patients' spirits.

Margaret's ambitions have only grown since her time as a girl in her troop. She earned her master's degree and now works as a book editor and marketing coordinator for Woodhall Press. She also finally achieved her childhood dream of becoming an author. Her memoir, *Bold, Brave, and Breathless*, tells the story of her childhood, her disability, and her journey of overcoming loss. She finds it incredibly powerful when readers reach out to her through her website to share their own struggles with inclusion and acceptance. For Margaret, these messages create a dialogue that can help strategize how to make the world a better place.

Even her hobbies are a testament to her Yes You Can spirit. Margaret is an athlete who runs in 5Ks and triathlons using her walker. She was named the Athlete of the Year for Achilles Connecticut, an adaptive sports team. When she sees the finish line in the distance, she says she feels a transformation inside her that shakes off the fatigue and allows her to sprint to the end. Whether she is pursuing her PhD, teaching, or writing her next book, Margaret continues to challenge the physical and social limitations that others try to place on her. She is a girl who turned her own life into a blueprint for resilience.

Margaret's journey is one of profound transformation, where she continually refines her purpose and strength. Just as extreme heat or pressure can refine raw materials into something enduring and beautiful, the intense challenges Margaret faced: the loss of her father and the stereotypes imposed by others, have forged her into the leader she is today. She continues to prove that while obstacles are inevitable, they are simply invitations to demonstrate that yes, you can.

Chapter 11
World Behind the Blur

Rebekkah Baccus (Ep 111)

When Sight Isn't Clear

Rebekkah Baccus learned very early that the world does not look the same to everyone. While other toddlers were busy chasing butterflies with perfect focus, Rebekkah was navigating a world that was permanently out of alignment. At just sixteen months old, she was diagnosed with amblyopia and strabismus, two conditions that made it difficult for her eyes to work together correctly. For years, she managed her vision as best she could, but life threw a devastating curveball when she was eleven years old. A horrific eye infection tore through her system, causing her vision to decrease significantly and leaving her to struggle with daily tasks that her peers took for granted.

Growing up with a visual impairment wasn't just a medical battle; it was a social one. Rebekkah was bullied by classmates who didn't understand why her eyes were different or why she moved the way she did. People even went so far as to tell her she would never reach normal milestones, like driving a car. These words hurt, but they also planted a seed of fierce determination. She found a hero in influencer Molly Burke, who lost her sight as a teenager. Rebekkah found herself drawn to Molly's story because they shared a similar timeline of vision loss.

As Rebekkah moved into her teenage years, she received a sobering prediction from her doctors. By the time she reaches twenty-five, macular degeneration will likely take its final toll, leaving her unable to drive and completely visually impaired. Instead of letting this countdown crush her spirit, Rebekkah decided to use her time and her voice to change how her community viewed disability. She knew that after completing her Bronze Award and Silver Award in her younger years, she was ready for a massive mission. She wanted to create an immersive experience that would allow people of all ages and backgrounds to step into her shoes, or rather, behind her glasses. She decided to call her project Through the Eyes, a quest to turn a personal struggle into a public lesson in empathy and awareness.

The Mountain Of Rejection

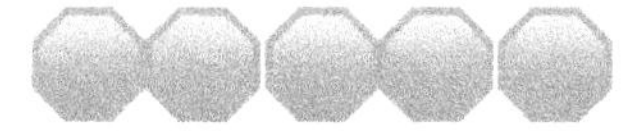

Turning a vision into a reality is never a straight path, and Rebekkah soon found herself climbing a mountain of no. Her first idea was to create a large, tactile sensory board that would be mounted permanently on a wall. She imagined it as a four-way block system, like a children's toy, where people could touch different textures and learn through their fingertips. She worked closely with her neighbor, an Occupational Therapy specialist, to design the concept. She proposed the idea to her eye doctor's office, the place she thought was the most logical home for the project, but then the world changed.

The 2020 pandemic hit with full force, throwing her plans into total shambles. Suddenly, placing a hands-on, high-touch exhibit in a medical clinic was no longer safe or viable. She had to redesign the entire plan, she realized as the shutdowns continued. She tried to pivot to the local library in Richmond Hill. Still, she encountered another unexpected roadblock: the library was beginning a massive renovation and couldn't accept her project during construction.

The technical rejections from locations were hard, but the feedback from the project committee was even harder to hear. When first presenting the modified plan, her leaders told her the project "wasn't big enough". They didn't doubt the quality of her idea, but they wanted her to push the boundaries of her leadership and impact. Rebekkah admitted that these roadblocks made her feel low at times, and she even asked her mother if they could just stop doing the sessions altogether when turnout felt uncertain. But she persisted. She refused to let no define her mission. She realized she had to advocate for her project the same way she had for her own eyesight, and she began building a new, even more ambitious plan that would eventually blow the skeptics away.

Science Of Sensory Learning

Rebekkah transitioned from a wall-poster idea to a full-scale immersive table. This change was key to making her project more portable and interactive. She became a manager, taking full control of the logistics and the budget. She spent her days as a homeschooled student, using her flexible hours to lead weekly meetings, draft outlines of every point she wanted to cover, and ensure her team stayed on track.

To carry out the Through the Eyes experience, Rebekkah had to think like an engineer and a teacher at once. She went on a massive shopping trip to Walmart, carefully budgeting for supplies and choosing the most cost-effective materials without sacrificing quality. She even had to sit at the table and measure the distance from her face to the surface to determine the exact length of the metal ball chains she would need to attach her simulation glasses, so that visitors could pick them up easily, but couldn't walk away with them.

The execution of the project relied on several innovative tools and partnerships that Rebekkah managed through her leadership:

- **Tactile Braille Learning:** She used a six-bump muffin tin and six balls to create a giant, hands-on Braille cell, allowing kids to recreate the letters they saw on the alphabet board.

- **Visual Simulation**: She hand-painted several pairs of glasses to simulate specific conditions, such as glaucoma, macular degeneration, and amblyopia, so her parents' friends could see exactly what it feels like to have no vision in one eye.

- **Digital Sustainability**: Instead of using paper flyers or business cards that would end up in the trash, she added QR codes that linked directly to her Weebly website and social media pages.

- **Accessibility Integration**: She specifically visited her local library to document their large-print books and specialized reading machines, which she included as resources for her visitors.

Rebekkah was meticulous about the details. She spent hours applying shelf paper to the sides of her table, redoing it four or five times because she couldn't stand it when the vinyl got crinkled. She wanted everything to be perfect for the grand opening, knowing that this project was her one chance to make a lasting statement. She was no longer just a student with a vision impairment; she was a producer of a community-wide educational event.

Moments Of Clarity

Opening day at the Jacob Grant Community Center was a whirlwind of activity. Rebekkah had spent weeks obsessively managing her social media accounts, posting on the community page to drum up interest. Her hard work paid off when eighty-five people walked through the doors to experience her project. She stood by her table with a tick counter, clicking it for every single visitor who came to learn.

The reactions she received were a mix of shock and profound connection. Many of her own family members and distant cousins had seen her posts on social media and realized for the first time just how much she had been suffering in silence. They reached out to tell her the project was inspiring and donated money to help cover her website and Facebook ad costs. The most heartwarming moments came from the children. When they put on the glasses and realized how she saw the world, they would exclaim, "Oh, this is what my friend sees, too!" Rebekkah would then ask for their names and help them spell them in the giant muffin-tin Braille, creating a memory that would stick with them far longer than a textbook lesson.

The impact of her project traveled far beyond the community center walls. Because she utilized social media so effectively, her project reached people in states across the country, proving that a girl in Georgia could educate someone in Wisconsin. Even the project leaders who had originally doubted her were blown away by the gorgeous project she had built. They were so impressed that they suggested she contact local news outlets to share her work. Rebekkah had successfully proven that her project wasn't just big enough; it was monumental. She had turned a potential ending (her vision loss) into a powerful beginning for hundreds of people who now looked at visual impairment with a sense of understanding rather than confusion.

Forging A Future

Completing this project changed the way Rebekkah viewed herself as a leader. She learned that she was a perfectionist who didn't like it when things got messed up, but she also discovered that she was a capable manager who could lead a team through a year of roadblocks. Her experience with the project even helped her in her high school jobs, where she used the management skills she honed during her mission. Her council was so impressed with her social media expertise that they even let her take over the accounts for a major regional festival called QuestFest.

Today, Rebekkah continues to use her voice and her experiences to prepare for her future. Although she is still driving for now, she is realistic about the changes to her vision. She remains active in spreading awareness, leading her peers in accessible-friendly activities, and continuing to share her story on digital platforms. She credits Girl Scouts with providing her with the foundation in public speaking and leadership that she uses every day. She even had the chance to partner with other influencers to amplify her message, realizing that "if you don't ask a question, the answer is always no."

Her advice to other girls starting their own major mission is to find a topic you are truly passionate about, because that passion is what will keep you writing when you want to quit. Rebekkah's journey taught her that even when the world seems to be fading into a blur, a clear purpose can act as a lighthouse. She didn't just build a sensory table; she built a bridge of empathy that will stand long after she can no longer see it. She proved that while her eyesight might be limited, her vision for a better world is limitless.

Rebekkah's project is like a carefully crafted lens: she took the cloudy, distorted perceptions that people had about visual impairment and used her own experiences to grind and polish them into a crystal-clear window of understanding, ensuring that anyone who looks through her work can finally see the beauty and the strength hidden within the struggle.

Chapter 12
Project Save the Girl Child

Himani Kalra (Ep 119)

The Prayer For A Son

Himani Kalra grew up in a household where she was very aware of her place in the world. As the second daughter in an Asian household, she didn't just hear the stories of gender preference; she lived through the subtle whispers and the explicit prayers of relatives and friends. When her parents were expecting her, she later learned that people often said, "We'll pray that you have a boy." This mindset, that a son was a blessing and a daughter was something to be settled for, was a deep-seated part of the cultural fabric she navigated every day. Her grandparents were doctors in India who treated patients in impoverished slum districts, and during her summer visits, Himani would often accompany them. There, she saw a stark reality: girls were kept at home to do housework and chores, while boys were sent off to school to build a future.

These experiences planted a seed of discomfort in Himani's heart, but the spark that finally ignited her mission came from a news story much closer to her home in Georgia. In 2018, a newborn baby girl, later named Baby India, was found wrapped in plastic and abandoned in a trash can only five miles from where Himani lived. This wasn't happening halfway across the globe in a developing nation; it was happening in her own backyard. This local tragedy proved that the preference for male children was a global issue of staggering proportions. Himani learned that female gendercide, the systematic termination of baby girls through abortion, poisoning, or deliberate neglect, is estimated to have claimed more lives than World War I and World War II combined.

She realized that someone needed to take charge and create a platform for change. She couldn't ignore the fact that in many societies, girls were simply not valued as much as boys. People saw less potential in their daughters and chose not to invest in their education or careers. Driven by a desire to uplift the status of girls and dismantle this harmful mindset, Himani decided to launch Project Save the Girl Child. Her goal was twofold: to educate the public about the existence of gendercide against women and to empower girls through direct access to education and healthcare. She was determined to prove that every girl has as much potential as any son in society.

Secret Hidden In Plain Sight

Stepping into the role of a leader for such a sensitive cause was not easy. Himani was a high school student trying to tackle a topic that most adults were too uncomfortable to mention. One of her biggest challenges was the cultural and political sensitivity. In India, female gendercide is a known problem, but it is often swept under the rug, and it is incredibly difficult to get people to talk about it honestly. In America, the challenge was the opposite: most people couldn't even fathom that such an issue existed in the modern world.

Furthermore, the project touched on topics like abortion, which is one of the most politically charged subjects in the United States. Himani had to navigate these waters with extreme care, ensuring that her message remained focused on the value and safety of the girl child without letting the project get derailed by political arguments. As a young person, she also struggled to find organizations that were willing to take her message seriously. When she began her research, she found that there were almost no youth-led organizations working to combat gendercide against women. This meant she had to build her own credibility from scratch and find partners who would trust a teenager to handle such a heavy burden.

Despite these hurdles, Himani remained confident that she would finish what she started. She used her resilience to push through the moments of doubt. She knew that her voice was needed precisely because it was the voice of a teen speaking to a teen, which can often make a much deeper impact than an adult delivering a lecture. She learned that to make a difference, she had to be more than just a volunteer; she had to be a persistent advocate. She spent hours on tedious research, finding the right emails, and calling professionals until she found the connections who could help her spread her message. She realized that while the topic was difficult, the silence was more dangerous, and she was the one who had to break it.

Literacy, Logic, And Love

Turning her passion into a practical project required extensive planning and a strong team of supporters. Himani knew that education was the most powerful tool she had to uplift girls and change their families' mindsets. She didn't want to just talk about the problem; she wanted to be part of the solution. She began holding gender awareness seminars at Asian cultural centers to educate parents and community members about the consequences of gendercide on the global population. She also worked to distribute brochures in the very slum districts of India she had visited with her grandparents, reaching families in high-risk domestic situations.

Her project expanded significantly when she began looking for ways to support girls who were already in vulnerable positions. She partnered with Send International, an organization that helped her connect with Afghan refugee families living in Clarkston, Georgia. Clarkston hosted a refugee resettlement area where families were often wary of outsiders. To gain their trust and provide a tangible benefit to the girls, Himani had to be incredibly organized and professional.

To carry out the project with high quality and long-term sustainability, she followed several essential operational steps:

- **Partnered** with the Invisible Girl Project to help rescue and resettle girls in India who were at risk of domestic termination.

- **Designed** a specialized STEM and classical reading curriculum to provide direct educational support to refugee daughters.

- **Recruited** and managed a team of 75 volunteers to assist with outreach and administrative tasks.

- **Established** herself as a Youth Brand Ambassador for her partner organizations to maintain a permanent platform for advocacy.

Himani's work with the Afghan refugee girls was particularly meaningful. She used her self-designed curriculum to teach them skills that would help them succeed in their new country, showing them that their education was an investment worth making. She realized that by giving these girls the tools to succeed, she was helping them break the shackles of poverty and gender-based limitations that had defined their families' lives for generations.

She wasn't just teaching them to read; she was teaching them that they had value. Every session she held was a step toward building a community where a daughter's potential was celebrated rather than ignored.

Letters From 75 Hearts

The impact of Project Save the Girl Child was visible in the measurable results Himani achieved throughout her journey. One of the most heartwarming parts of her project involved her team of 75 volunteers. Together, they wrote almost 450 letters of support to the girls rescued through the Invisible Girl Project in India. These weren't just pieces of paper; they were messages of encouragement that showed these survivors that they were loved, valued, and meant so much to society. Himani realized that these letters were a vital part of the healing process, helping the girls see themselves as more than just victims.

Her role as a Youth Brand Ambassador for the Invisible Girl Project allowed her to take her advocacy to a national level. She was no longer just a girl with a local project; she was a representative for a global movement. Her work helped bring international attention to the crisis of gender preference that experts were beginning to call a gendercide epidemic. The feedback she received from the community was overwhelmingly positive, and she was shocked to see how far her message could reach through the power of social media and networking.

One of the most fulfilling moments occurred with an update regarding the story of Baby India, the infant found near her home. The authorities finally found the family and the mother who had abandoned the child. While Himani hadn't worked on that specific case directly, seeing the community now recognize and act on these issues gave her a profound sense of hope. It proved that people were waking up to the injustices she had been fighting against. Her project had created a blueprint for a solution that others could now follow to address similar needs in their own backyards or even across the globe. She had successfully moved the needle from ignorance toward awareness, one seminar and one letter at a time.

The Legacy Of The Second Daughter

Completing this massive project was a transformational experience that provided Himani with a stellar education in leadership. She learned that being a leader meant being an advocate, a manager, and a researcher all at once. Her final report for the project was almost 60 pages long, which she described as being like writing a mini thesis. The process taught her how to write a formal proposal, interview professionals, and lead a diverse team of volunteers toward a common goal. These were skills that many people don't master until they are well into their professional careers.

The honor of being named a National Gold Award Girl Scout for her project was a moment she would never forget. It was a personal achievement that rewarded years of hard work and validated her passion for the cause. She realized that the project allowed her to better herself and her community through her own creativity and drive. She transitioned from being a girl who listened to others' opinions of her value to a woman who used her voice to define her own purpose. She learned that no matter how daunting a journey seems at first, it always gets easier if you have a mission you truly believe in.

Today, Himani is continuing her adventure in New York City, where she is attending college and looking for new ways to expand Save the Girl Child. New York offers a diverse community of immigrants and refugees, providing her with even more opportunities to partner with organizations and touch lives. She plans to keep her organization growing in Atlanta, India, and now New York, ensuring that her legacy of service continues long after her official project ended. She encourages every girl to find a cause she is interested in and see how far they can take it, because the impact will often go far beyond what they ever expected.

Himani's journey is like a single candle lit in a vast, dark cavern: while the darkness of gender preference and gendercide seemed overwhelming at first, her small flame of awareness drew others to her side, creating a glowing path of hope and education that now illuminates the futures of hundreds of girls, ensuring their worth is never again left in the shadows of the past.

Chapter 13
Heart of Belonging

Tapestry of Inclusion

As you have journeyed through these chapters, you have witnessed the transformative power of a single person who decides that inclusion is worth the effort. You saw how a secret lunchbox led to a published book celebrating cultural diversity, and how a diagnosis of autism became the foundation for a Sensory Friendly Future for an entire community. You read about the courage required to talk about the heavy, unspoken weight of mental health stigma and the leadership it took to build a high-end boutique so foster youth could shop with "their heads held high". Each of these stories is a thread in a larger tapestry of transformation, proving that whether you are building a hydroponic wall or fighting female gendercide, the heart of the work is the same: ensuring every person is seen, heard, and valued.

Refining the Leader Within

These narratives weren't just about the awards; they were about the girls' internal growth. You learned that being braver than you believe often means pushing through a mountain of red tape or facing a wall of no when people tell you that your dreams are off-limits. You saw leaders pivot during global pandemics, turning in-person workshops into virtual soapboxes that reached people across the country. This journey from being quiet and shy to becoming a vocal advocate is your professional roadmap. You are not a bystander; you are a source of vital, life-saving information waiting to be released. Whatever gap in belonging makes your heart yearn for change is the very thing that should drive your next steps.

The Inclusion Toolkit:
A Guide to Building Bridges

Using your voice for inclusion requires a blend of passion, strategy, and technical skill. To help you launch your own mission, use these steps drawn from the successful projects in this book:

- **Step 1:** Identify the Barrier. Look for the silence in your community. Ask: Who is missing from the table? Is it someone with a physical disability, a foster teen, or a student who feels invisible because of their culture?

- **Step 2:** Conduct Deep-Dive Research. Find the "how" behind your "why". Dig into statistics on suicide rates, identify hidden indicators, or learn the logistics and language of gallery curation.

- **Step 3:** Build Your Diverse Dream Team. You cannot do this alone. Reach out to key parts of your community: principals, nutritionists, or directors. Find a mentor who will help you move forward when you feel overwhelmed.

- **Step 4:** Design the Blueprint for Accessibility. Create a curriculum or physical structure that makes your message taken seriously. Use professional tools like Canva for catalogs, Amazon Publishing for books, or high-end filming equipment for educational videos.

- **Step 5:** Make the Heart-to-Heart Connection. People want to see your personal connection to the project. Whether it's crying with a family who feels seen or sharing your own lived experience with a disability, your vulnerability is your greatest strength.

- **Step 6**: Navigate the Logistics. Manage your budget through resourceful workarounds, like guessing the email formats of executives when you can't find contact info or writing grants to purchase equipment.

Sustaining the Movement

A true leader ensures their project outlasts their direct involvement. To make your inclusion mission permanent, focus on sustainability:

- **Create Permanent Resources:** Host your curriculum in a digital ecosystem or Google folder so others can continue the lessons after you move on. Find a partner to maintain the resource.

- **Draft Formal Agreements:** Like a pre-law professional, create agreements with the organizations you work with to ensure your resources are maintained.

- **Share Your Blueprint:** Don't just finish; give your project to the world. Use QR codes or social media to share your global impact and help others recreate your success in their own neighborhoods.

Your Journey is Just Beginning

The more time and energy you put into your mission, the more you will change as a person.

You will learn how to hustle, communicate with people from different backgrounds, and turn a moment of rejection into a standing ovation that changes the world. Your voice is like a seed that can grow into a forest of hope. You are standing at a launchpad, ready to build your own bridge of belonging.

♡ The world needs your unique flavor. It is time to speak up. ♡

ABOUT THE AUTHOR

Sheryl M. Robinson is a podcaster, mentor, and speaker dedicated to helping teens and young adults discover their unique gifts, talents, and abilities, creating a path toward their dreams.

Sheryl holds a Master of Arts in Servant Leadership from Viterbo University and a Bachelor's in Accounting from Southern Illinois University – Carbondale. She has been a proud member of Girl Scouts for more than 30 years. Her passion for supporting teens, especially those pursuing the Girl Scout Gold Award, led her to create *Hearts of Gold*, a YouTube series and podcast featuring Gold Award Girl Scouts from across the world.

In recognition of her work elevating and supporting the Girl Scout Highest Awards, Sheryl has been honored with the GSUSA Thanks II Award, the organization's highest recognition for service.

Recognizing the need for younger Girl Scouts to have resources and role models as they pursue the Bronze Award and Silver Award, Sheryl created this middle-grade book series to share inspiring stories of leadership, courage, and community change.

She deeply believes that the Girl Scout Highest Awards not only make the world a better place but also transform the Girl Scouts who earn them into building lifelong changemakers, confident problem-solvers, and compassionate leaders.

ACKNOWLEDGMENTS

Creating this book has been a journey shaped by many remarkable people, and I am deeply grateful for each of you.

To **my mom, Jean**, who first started me in Girl Scouts many years ago and planted the seeds of everything that would follow.

To **my daughter, Nikki**, a Bronze, Silver, and Gold Award Girl Scout whose dedication inspires me every day. Watching you flourish through each phase of your life is one of my greatest joys.

To **my husband, Mark,** thank you for always supporting me and the many plates you quietly set beside me while I typed away. I thank God for bringing you into my life every day.

To **all the Gold Award Girl Scouts** who have shared their stories on the Hearts of Gold podcast. Thank you for trusting me with your journeys. Your courage, creativity, and leadership inspire thousands.

To the **Girl Scout leaders, volunteers, and parents** who support these incredible young women: your encouragement makes meaningful change possible.

To **Cassie**, who encouraged me to restart my Girl Scout journey when my daughter joined Girl Scouts.

A heartfelt thank you to **Stacie and Shannan**, who have listened to me talk about this book for years and never stopped encouraging me to make it happen.

To **Walter**, my podcast editor for the first nine years, and **Tommy**, my new editor, and to their entire family, especially **Greg**, whose podcasting challenge a decade ago helped set all of this into motion.

And finally, to **Elsie, Rob, Cliff, Daniel, and Jessica**: thank you for your inspiration, for keeping the process fun, for sharing your knowledge, and for helping Hearts of Gold continue to grow.

This project exists because of each of you.
Thank you for helping bring these stories to life.

To all the future Bronze, Silver, and Gold Award Girl Scouts and others inspired by this book. Be the change you want to see in the world and remember your leadership matters.

MORE STORIES

Want to hear more inspiring stories from Gold Award Girl Scouts?

HeartsofGoldPodcast.com

You can watch or listen to new episodes every month.

Podcast:
https://bit.ly/3JT7x0w

YouTube:
https://bit.ly/3P5nns8

Instagram:
https://bit.ly/3JZ2JX8